JORDAN SPIETH

BY TYLER MASON

SportsZone

An Imprint of Abdo Publishing
abdopublishing.com

abdopublishing.com

Published by Abdo Publishing, a division of ABDO, PO Box 398166, Minneapolis, Minnesota 55439. Copyright © 2018 by Abdo Consulting Group, Inc. International copyrights reserved in all countries. No part of this book may be reproduced in any form without written permission from the publisher. SportsZone™ is a trademark and logo of Abdo Publishing.

Printed in the United States of America, North Mankato, Minnesota
052017
092017

THIS BOOK CONTAINS
RECYCLED MATERIALS

Cover Photo: Andrew Dieb/Icon Sportswire/AP Images
Interior Photos: Andrew Dieb/Icon Sportswire/AP Images, 1; Matt Slocum/AP Images, 4–5, 25; Philippe Millereau/DPPI/Icon Sportswire, 7; Tony Gutierrez/AP Images, 9; Steve Sisney/The Oklahoman/AP Images, 10–11; Romeo Guzman/Cal Sport Media/AP Images, 13; Reed Saxon/AP Images, 14; LM Otero/AP Images, 16–17; Charlie Neibergall/AP Images, 19; Darron Cummings/AP Images, 20; Rick Rycroft/AP Images, 22–23; Ken Murray/Icon Sportswire/AP Images, 26; Charlie Riedel/AP Images, 29

Editor: Todd Kortemeier
Series Designer: Craig Hinton

Publisher's Cataloging-in-Publication Data

Names: Mason, Tyler, author.
Title: Jordan Spieth : golf sensation / by Tyler Mason.
Other titles: Golf sensation
Description: Minneapolis, MN : Abdo Publishing, 2018. | Series: Playmakers | Includes bibliographical references and index.
Identifiers: LCCN 2017930232 | ISBN 9781532111518 (lib. bdg.) | ISBN 9781680789362 (ebook)
Subjects: LCSH: Spieth, Jordan, 1993- --Juvenile literature. | Golfers --United States--Biography--Juvenile literature.
Classification: DDC 796.352 [B]--dc23
LC record available at http://lccn.loc.gov/2017930232

TABLE OF CONTENTS

Jordan Spieth

CHAPTER 1

THE MASTER

A t a time when many 21-year-olds are still in college, Jordan Spieth was making himself a household name.

Spieth was just 21 when he won the 2015 Masters Tournament. He tied a record for the best score at the famous event. Spieth finished 18 shots under par. That tied Tiger Woods's record from 1997. Spieth received the famous green jacket given to all Masters winners. He also got a place in the history books.

Jordan Spieth celebrates winning the 2015 Masters.

The Masters is one of golf's four major tournaments. Spieth's 2015 performance there made him an instant star. He had played some of the best golf in Masters history. Spieth led for all four days of the event. It was the first time any player had done that since 1976. The win was only the start of Spieth's promising career. It took a lot of hard work to get to that point.

Jordan Spieth was also really good at baseball. Spieth played on very competitive teams. He was a left-handed pitcher. But he golfs right-handed.

Jordan Spieth grew up in Dallas, Texas. He played more than just golf as a kid. Jordan's favorite sport was baseball. But he quit playing when he was 12. He did that to focus on golf.

Jordan comes from a family of athletes. His mom played basketball in college. His dad was a college baseball player.

Jordan played in the 2007 Evian Masters Jr. Cup in France as a 13-year-old.

Jordan's brother, Steven, played basketball at Brown University. Jordan also played basketball and football as a kid.

Jordan was around eight years old when he started playing golf at Brookhaven Country Club in Dallas. Other Professional Golfers' Association (PGA) golfers learned to play at that course.

The way Jordan holds the club is unusual. He's done it ever since he was a kid. Most golfers use what is called an overlap grip. Jordan's grip is similar. But he does not put his right pinkie over his left pointer finger. Instead, his left pointer finger goes over his right hand. It is a different grip than what most golfers use. But it works well for Jordan.

It didn't take long for Jordan to have success at golf. He shot a 63 when he was 12 years old. He later won the US Junior Amateur Championship. He was just 15.

Jordan had to miss his high school graduation. He was playing in the Byron Nelson Championship on the PGA Tour. Jordan was just 17 years old. He tied for 32nd place.

Jordan hits out of the sand at the 2010 Byron Nelson Championship.

Jordan won the event again two years later. He was the second player to win it twice. Tiger Woods was the other, but he had won three.

In 2011, Jordan made the US Walker Cup team. The Walker Cup pits the best amateurs in the US against the best from Great Britain and Ireland. Jordan and the US lost.

But it was clear that Jordan had talent. His early success was a sign of things to come.

Jordan Spieth

CHAPTER 2

LONG-HITTING LONGHORN

Jordan Spieth was the top-ranked high school golfer in the country. College teams were lining up to get him.

Spieth chose to attend the University of Texas in 2011. The school is located in the state capital of Austin. It is less than a three-hour drive from his hometown of Dallas. People expected big things from Spieth in college. He quickly began living up to expectations.

Spieth hits off the tee while playing with the Texas Longhorns in 2012.

He was ranked eighth on *Golf World*'s "Top 50 College Players to Watch" list as a freshman. Spieth tied for sixth place in his first college tournament. His performance helped Texas win the overall team championship of the event.

Spieth had many college offers to choose from. Some schools had their eyes on him for a long time. Spieth's coach at Texas was John Fields. Spieth was 11 years old when Fields saw him play for the first time.

Spieth finished second in the Jack Nicklaus Invitational. The tournament was held on the course in Ohio that was designed by the acclaimed golfer. The only player to beat Spieth was Thomas Pieters. Pieters played for the University of Illinois. Spieth lost by two strokes. Pieters also became a pro golfer.

Texas was ranked number one in the country. Spieth played a big part in the Longhorns' success. He later became Texas's top golfer.

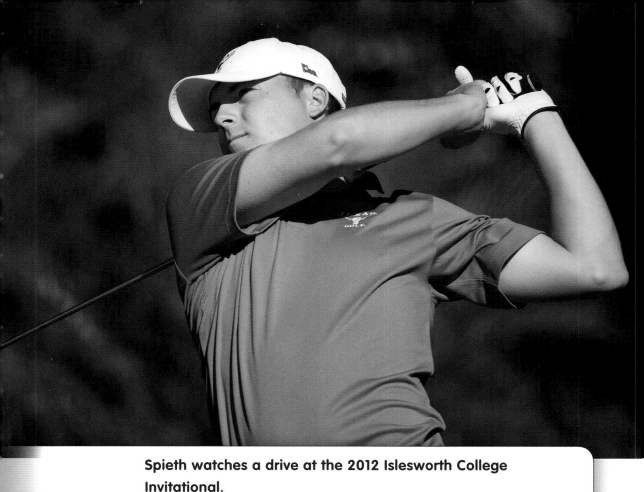

Spieth watches a drive at the 2012 Islesworth College Invitational.

Spieth also played on the PGA Tour during college. He had to compete as an amateur. That meant he did not accept any money. Spieth played in the Northern Trust Open and the Valero Texas Open in college. He missed the cut at the Northern Trust Open. Spieth did make the cut at the Valero Texas Open. He finished in a tie for 41st.

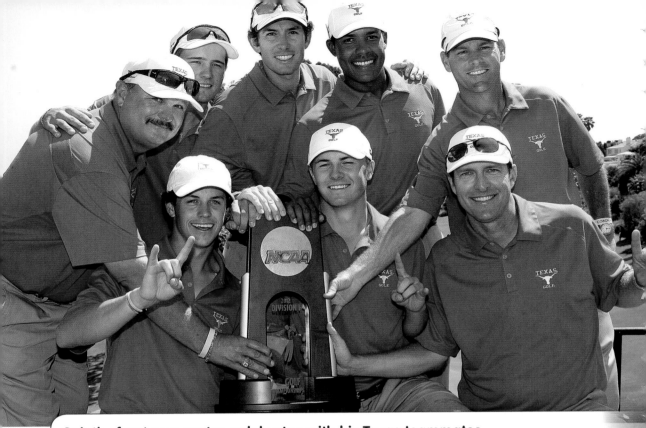

Spieth, *front row center*, celebrates with his Texas teammates after winning the national title.

Texas had gone 40 years between national championships in golf. That changed when Spieth arrived. The Longhorns' last college golf title was in 1972. Spieth helped end that streak as a freshman in 2012.

The Longhorns played the University of Alabama for the 2012 championship. The event was held in California. It was played at Riviera Country Club.

Five players from each team played an opponent from the other team. Spieth was matched up against Alabama's Justin Thomas. Spieth won his match in the final round. Texas won 3–2 over the Crimson Tide.

Spieth is one of several PGA golfers to have played at Texas. Tom Kite and Ben Crenshaw are two of the more famous Longhorns. Pro golfers Justin Leonard, Brandel Chamblee, and Brad Elder also played for Texas.

The Golf Coaches Association of America gave Spieth several honors. He was named to the All-Freshmen team. Spieth was also a first-team All-American.

The Big 12 Conference also honored Spieth. He was the Big 12 Player of the Year for the 2011–12 season.

Spieth's college career didn't last long. He left school during his sophomore year in 2012–13. Spieth was on his way to the PGA Tour.

16   *Jordan Spieth*

CHAPTER 3

A TOUR PRO

Jordan Spieth was a teenager when he turned pro. He announced his decision on December 14, 2012. Spieth was 19 years old. The decision meant he would leave Texas during his sophomore year.

It didn't take long for Spieth to shine as a pro. He finished tied for second place in his third event after college. That was at the Puerto Rico Open. He tied for seventh at the Tampa Bay Championship one

Spieth lines up a putt at the Colonial in 2013.

week later. Spieth already had two top-10 finishes in his first three months as a pro.

Spieth won his first PGA Tour event before he turned 20. The 19-year-old won the John Deere Classic in July 2013. That made him the youngest PGA Tour winner in 82 years. The win did not come easily. Spieth started the last round six shots behind the leader. But he rallied with birdies on five of the last six holes.

Spieth played in three of golf's four majors in 2013. He shot 10-over par in the British Open. That tied him for 44th. Spieth missed the cut at both the US Open and PGA Championship that year.

Spieth made a chip shot from a sand trap on the final hole. He later called it the luckiest shot of his life. That put him into a playoff. He faced Zach Johnson and David Hearn. All three players were still tied after four playoff holes. Spieth made a par on the fifth hole to win his first event.

Spieth holds the championship trophy after winning the 2013 John Deere Classic.

The John Deere Classic win earned Spieth $828,000. It also earned him a spot as a PGA Tour regular member. He was only a temporary member coming into the tournament. Spieth had

Spieth signs autographs for fans at the 2013 Presidents Cup.

two more second-place finishes in 2013. He also finished fourth at the Deutsche Bank Championship.

The 2013 season was an impressive one for Spieth. He started out the year ranked 810th in the world. He finished it ranked 20th and was the PGA Tour Rookie of the Year. Spieth had nine finishes in the top 10. He also made nearly $4 million in 2013.

Spieth wasn't done. He made the US team that played in the Presidents Cup. The Presidents Cup matches the US against a team from the rest of the world minus Europe. His selection was a surprise. Spieth was the youngest player ever to play for the United States. He was just 20 years old. Spieth was also the first PGA Tour rookie in a Presidents Cup. Team captain Fred Couples selected him.

Michael Greller is Spieth's caddie. He first worked with Spieth at the 2011 US Junior Amateur tournament. Greller was a sixth-grade math teacher in Seattle. He became Spieth's full-time caddie in 2012.

The United States won the 2013 Presidents Cup. It beat the international team by three points. The win was the latest achievement for Spieth. His first year on tour was a good one. The next few years would be even better.

Jordan Spieth

CHAPTER 4

BREAKING OUT

Jordan Spieth had a strong rookie year. He followed it up with two wins in 2014. However, Spieth's breakout year came in 2015.

Spieth had finished second in the Masters in 2014. He won the famous event one year later. It was an easy victory for the young star. He led by four

Spieth kisses his putter after winning the 2014 Australian Open.

strokes going into the final day of the event. Spieth won by four shots over Phil Mickelson and Justin Rose.

> Spieth won five events in 2015. They earned him lots of money. He was named the 2015 PGA Tour Player of the Year. It was the first time he had won the award as golf's top player.

It was a historic performance for Spieth. The 21-year-old was the second-youngest Masters winner ever. The only younger winner was Tiger Woods. Spieth was dominant. He led after each round of play.

Spieth followed up his win at the Masters with another major victory. He won the US Open at Chambers Bay in Washington two months later. That win was more dramatic than his Masters victory. Dustin Johnson could have beaten Spieth on the final hole.

The 2014 Masters winner Bubba Watson, *left*, presents Spieth with the famous green jacket for winning the 2015 Masters.

Spieth, *right*, and caddie Michael Greller discuss an upcoming shot at the 2015 Byron Nelson Championship.

Johnson needed to make his 12-foot (3.7-m) putt to win. He missed. But he still could force a playoff. He missed again. Spieth was the US Open champion. He was the youngest golfer to win the tournament since 1923.

Spieth earned $3.6 million for winning the Masters and the US Open. He was the sixth golfer ever to win both events in the same year. Spieth also won the John Deere Classic in 2015. That was the same event he won for his first PGA Tour victory. He later won the 2015 TOUR Championship to complete his successful year. He also became the top-ranked player in the world.

Spieth is already one of the highest-paid golfers in the PGA. He won $23 million from events in 2015. He made even more from endorsements and appearances. He earned an estimated total of $50 million in 2015.

Spieth had a strong 2015 season. That allowed him to play in the 2016 Ryder Cup, held in Minnesota. This event pits the top US golfers against the top European golfers every two years. Spieth and the US team won the cup back from Europe on home soil. It was their first win since 2008.

Spieth had the chance to play in the Olympics in 2016. He turned down the opportunity. The 2016 Olympics were held in Rio de Janeiro, Brazil. Many golfers did attend. England's Justin Rose won the gold medal.

Spieth has accomplished a lot on the course. That has helped him be successful outside of golf. He started the Jordan Spieth Family Foundation. The foundation raises money for families in need. That includes children with special needs. Spieth's younger sister, Ellie, was born with a brain disorder. She was his inspiration for the foundation.

Spieth has a strong relationship with his sister. He brings her something from each trip he takes. Spieth said Ellie is the best thing that happened to his family. Spieth's foundation also helps military families. And it is involved in projects for youth golf. Spieth's foundation hopes to help more young kids play the game.

The first charity event for Spieth's foundation was in 2014. It was the Jordan Spieth Shootout and Concert. Country musician Jake Owen performed. The event raised almost $250,000.

Spieth celebrates making a putt during the final round of the 2016 Ryder Cup.

Spieth has also earned money from endorsements. The future looks bright for Spieth. At a young age, he had rewritten the record books several times. And it appears that more is to come for the talented golfer.

FUN FACTS AND QUOTES

- "This was arguably the greatest day of my life. To join Masters history and put my name on that trophy and to have this jacket forever, it's something that I can't fathom right now." —Spieth, after receiving his green jacket for winning the 2015 Masters

- "I love spending time with her. It's humbling to see the struggles she goes through each day that we take for granted. Because of Ellie, it has always been a priority to me to be in tune to the needs of others." —Spieth on his sister, Ellie, who has special needs due to her brain disorder

- Spieth started to change his diet as a pro golfer. He wanted to eat healthier. He now eats lots of vegetables even though he says he hates them. Spieth is also supposed to drink a certain amount of water while he is on the course.

- "Jordan is so beyond his years. I like everything about him. He's polite, he's humble, he handles himself so well, on and off the golf course. And he's obviously a wonderful player and now a Masters champion." —Golf legend Jack Nicklaus on Spieth after the 2015 Masters

WEBSITES

To learn more about Playmakers, visit **abdobooklinks.com**. These links are routinely monitored and updated to provide the most current information available.

GLOSSARY

amateur
Someone who is not paid to perform an activity.

birdie
A golf score in which a golfer finishes the hole one shot under par.

cut
When the number of players is reduced in a tournament, leaving only the players with the best scores to play the final rounds.

endorsement
When an athlete promotes a company in exchange for their products or money.

freshman
A first-year student.

major
Professional golf's four biggest events: the Masters, the US Open, the British Open, and the PGA Championship.

par
The number of shots golfers are expected to need to finish a hole.

putt
A golf stroke taken on the green. A golfer uses a special club, called a putter, for this shot.

rookie
A first-year player.

sand trap
A sand-filled obstacle, usually near greens.

stroke
Equal to one shot. The total number of strokes a golfer takes in a round is his or her score.

INDEX

FURTHER RESOURCES

Gifford, Clive. *Golf: From Tee to Green—The Essential Guide for Young Golfers.* New York: Kingfisher, 2013.

Gitlin, Marty. *Jordan Spieth: Golf Star.* Mankato, MN: North Star Editions, 2017.

Lemke, Christina. *Golf.* Vero Beach, FL: Rourke Educational Media, 2017.